Southern Italy Travel Guide 2023:

A Tour of the Mediterranean Beauty

Christopher Chako

Table of contents

Foreword

William set off on a voyage that would create immeasurable memories in the midst of the summer. The bustling city of Sicily in Southern Italy, Palermo, was his last stop. Palermo drew him in like a familiar friend with its long history and allure of the Mediterranean.

The city surrounded William in a swirl of hues, aromas, and noises as he walked into the cobblestone streets. Sicilian culture was shown in vivid detail in the throbbing marketplaces, which were brimming with the wealth of the land and sea. Savoring the island's gastronomic delights, he couldn't resist the allure of fresh cannoli and arancini.

He walked through the congested lanes being guided by the wind's whispers, discovering a different historical detail at every bend. While the ethereal beauty of the

Catacombs of the Capuchins served as a frightening reminder of death, the magnificence of the Palermo Cathedral astounded him. He was drawn into their world by the kindness of the villagers, whose jokes and tales actually touched his heart.

William set off on a voyage down the coast that was bathed in sunlight after leaving Palermo. His adventures were set against the peaceful background of the gorgeous Cefalu beaches and the little fishing communities of Sciacca and Trapani. It was as if the stones at the Valley of the Temples in Agrigento murmured stories of long-gone civilizations, taking him back in time.

William learned about the peaceful rhythm of rural life among the undulating hills and olive trees. He found a community ready to share their transformation from the shadows of the past in Corleone, a notoriously bad town that had undergone a humble transformation.

William left Southern Italy as his days there came to an end with more than just mementos; he also left with a heart that had been nourished by the genuineness of the place. His stay in Palermo and the surrounding area left an indelible impression on him that would compel him to return again and again to the place where Mediterranean culture, history, and friendships were rekindled in the embrace of time.

Warm greetings from southern Italy.

Markets

You'll like this book if you enjoy getting lost in the vibrant colors of street markets to learn about the customs, tastes, and fragrances of a city or country while also getting a glimpse of how its people live their daily lives.

San Gregorio Armeno Market in Naples

which is entirely dedicated to the presentation of its famed presepi or nativity scenes, is one Italian Street Market that is unlike any other in the world. Statues and figurines from the nativity scene, examples of exquisitely crafted antiques that have long been a must-see, may be seen as you stroll through the historic district's winding streets. The odd thing about this street market is that, although it is associated with the Christmas season, it is open all year long in Naples. Every day, its artists produce fresh shepherd figures that resemble prominent persons from local, national, and worldwide news.

The **Fera 'o Luni**, which translates to "the Monday fair" in English, is what they refer to, although this market, which has a long history and is held every day in Catania's Piazza Carlo Alberto, truly takes place every day. The Fera 'o Luni has been a source of joy for Catania residents since the time of the Spanish rule over the country; the only thing that has changed over the years is its location, which has moved from in front of the Basilica della Collegiata in Piazza Università to its current location. The Catania market is a veritable cacophony of sounds and colors right now, a sight for both locals and visitors alike who, as usual, are awestruck by the radiance and vibrancy of the Etnean people.

The **Capo and Ballar markets** in the lovely city of Palermo, Sicily, are a definite must-visit if you're seeking vibrant and hectic marketplaces. This provincial capital has long served as a key hub for Mediterranean trade, and today's Capo and Ballar markets not only provide fresh produce and vegetables from the region's farms but also give guests a fantastic taste of

Sicilian street food. The so-called rabbinate, the loud cries of the vendors who attempt to pique passers-by's interest in the markets by praising the quality and pricing of their wares in their distinct dialect, is what keeps people's attention.

Souvenir

Venetian masks

A wonderful memento to bring home from Italy is a Venetian mask, especially from Venice, where mask-making has a long history.

These ornately adorned masks have a long history in Venice, where they were worn during the Venice Carnival. The city's rich culture and history are honored during this event.

An unusual and one-of-a-kind Italy memento, each mask is handcrafted and distinctive.

Burano Lace

On the little island of Burano in the Venetian Lagoon, a traditional craft known as Burano lace was first created. Craftsmen who have been educated in the technique of making Burano lace make it by hand.

Utilizing age-old methods, the lace is created, yielding a stunning and one-of-a-kind item that is incomparable.

The exquisite motifs and delicate elegance of this delicate lace are known. In addition to tablecloths, curtains, apparel, and accessories, Burano lace has many more uses.

Murano Glass

On the island of Murano, which is close to Venice, incredible glass art may be seen. For generations, Murano's glassmakers have been honing their trade, and now, art enthusiasts and collectors from all over the globe clamor for their works.

Murano glass comes in a variety of hues and designs, from classic Venetian patterns to more contemporary, abstract pieces. Vases, bowls, jewelry, and figures are some of the top souvenirs made of Murano glass.

Buying Murano glass not only provides a lovely and one-of-a-kind keepsake, but it also helps the neighborhood's skilled craftspeople, who have been producing these magnificent pieces for generations. It's a lovely way to bring back a treasured piece of Italian artwork and culture.

Italian-made designer goods

World-renowned Italian fashion labels exist! Gucci and Fendi are two brands that I truly like. Popular designer brands include, among others, Zegna, Missoni, Dolce & Gabbana, Armani, Valentino, Versace, Prada, and Armani.

Pottery and Ceramics

Beautiful pottery or ceramics are great options if you want to bring home a one-of-a-kind, classic memento from Italy. There are several types and kinds of beautiful pottery produced in Italy, which has a long tradition in the art.

Take into account the style that most closely resembles your preferences and likes when purchasing ceramics or pottery. Look for artwork with typical Italian themes like olive trees or grapevines, or choose something more contemporary and abstract.

Perfume

The best method to bring back memories of a trip to Italy is via perfume. Some of the top names in the fragrance market are from Italy, which is well-known for its fragrances.

The same as the designer brands, you can get fragrances from Prada, Bottega Veneta, Armani, or Valentino. They provide a variety of unique and creative mixtures that will make you feel as if you are still in Italy even after you have left Italy.

Sample a variety of scents until you locate the one that best fits you as a technique to find the ideal smell.

Leather Made Goods
If you want to bring home something elegant and useful from Italy, think about buying leather products. Italian leather shoes, purses, wallets, belts, and jackets are just a few of the high-quality leather products that are produced in this nation and have a long history of being produced.
It might be expensive to purchase genuine Italian leather products. However, some goods might be made of fake leather or a different material, therefore it's crucial to check the quality.

All things considered, purchasing these well-made Italian trinkets is a lovely way to return home with an expensive and useful keepsake that will endure for years.

The Leather School is located in Florence and offers tours of the factory and lectures on the development of Italian leathercraft. Numerous locations, including marketplaces, street sellers, and upscale stores, carry leather items.

Religious artwork
Beautiful religious art may be found throughout Italy. Many old cathedrals and art galleries can be found in Rome and Naples, and they both contain lovely and genuine artwork.
Being respectful and conscious of the cultural and spiritual value of these works of religious art is crucial while acquiring them. Since many of these objects are holy, you should make sure you're buying them from

an ethical merchant that obtains them from reliable sources.

Buying religious art in Rome or Naples might serve as a memorable keepsake that will help you remember your trip and Italy's rich cultural and religious past. You'll discover something that appeals to your heart and soul among the numerous exquisite and genuine things available.

Availability of Religious Art

Religious art, including crucifixes, icons, and saint statues, are widely available in Rome's stores and marketplaces. Due to its abundance of art museums and galleries, Vatican City is a well-liked location for religious art.

There is a strong heritage of religious art in Naples, and there are several stores and galleries that offer beautiful works that include the Madonna, Jesus, and other religious figures. You may purchase handmade pastori or nativity sculptures in

Naples' San Gregorio Armeno, a special alley where you can get the ideal holiday Italian memento.

Gold and Silver Jewelry

Italy's eternal mementos include gold and silver jewelry. Italian jewelers have produced magnificent items of gold and silver jewelry for generations, each piece featuring minute workmanship and precision.

Every item of jewelry is distinctive, from statement necklaces to understated earrings and rings. There is an abundance of striking jewelry available in Italy, whether you're searching for a statement piece or something little and delicate to wear every day.

Italy's Jewellery Stores

Choosing a trustworthy merchant is crucial when buying gold and silver jewelry in Italy. A lot of businesses have centuries of experience and expertise in traditional arts, which they use to create the ideal piece of jewelry.

The gold jewelry is produced in Vicenza, an Italian city, which is well-known.

Italian espresso cups, cookbooks, a set of artisan knives, and tablecloths from Perugia are some more items you may purchase.

Nightlife

There is no better location to have a good time than Italy, whether you appreciate the party scene or prefer a relaxed wine bar where you can sip a glass of Brunello while spending quality time with a few friends. Italia's nightlife and culture are quite distinct from its daytime counterparts. Every big city has a distinctive nightlife that is unmatched anyplace in the globe after the sun goes down. So put your problems aside, get yourself a big glass of wine spritzer, go to a posh club in town, and spend the evening taking advantage of all that Italy's vibrant nightlife has to offer with your closest friends and some enjoyable music!

Milan, A Glamorous City

Milan is one of the most amazing places in Italy to visit if you want an outstanding nightlife experience. It is home to innumerable nightclubs that are among the greatest in the world. If you appreciate dancing, great wines, cocktails, and other beverages, this city is the ideal location for you. Milan is renowned for its enormous selection of pubs, lounges, and nightclubs, providing all the essentials for the best Italian nightlife. This is one of the top cities to visit if you're seeking Italy's greatest nightlife.

Places to Go: The greatest nightclubs in Milan include Hollywood Rythmoteque, The Doping Club, Monkey Cocktail Bar, Just Cavalli Milan, Backdoor 43, and H Club Diana.

Unlimited Live Entertainment in Rome

Italian nightlife Italy is a country you won't soon forget because of how vibrant it becomes when visitors arrive to take advantage of everything the city has to offer. Rome's nightlife is distinctive from that of most other cities in that it emphasizes the city's gastronomic delights and the consumption of great wines imported from all around Italy. In Rome, there are several places to go if you enjoy dance or electronic clubs.

The Testaccio neighborhood, renowned for its house music clubs, salsa discos, pubs, and other hot night places, are two locations you must visit. Piazza Navona is also a great choice for night owls with its cafés and wine bars. A speakeasy named Jerry Thomas Shari Vari - The Playhouse

A night of festivities in Florence

You may not immediately picture nightclubs and other places to party all night when you think of Florence, but you'd be surprised. There are many incredible spots in the lovely city where you can dance the night away while enjoying some excellent music. It's exhilarating and energizing to go out at night in Florence, Italy. If you want to enjoy amazing nightlife while on vacation in Italy, this is one of the greatest locations to visit.

These are the places you must go: The Blob Club, Moyo Bar, Space Club, Public House 27, Red Garter, Sverso, and The Joshua Tree Pub.

Versilia: The Finest Beach Get-togethers

Many young people from throughout the nation visit this region of Italy because of its vibrant nightlife. The finest beach parties in Italy can be found in Versilia. It is one of the must-visit spots for nightlife in Italy when you wish to have a unique nightlife experience because of the picturesque setting where some of the best disco clubs in the nation are located.

You Must Visit These Places: La Capannina di Franceschi, Seven Apples, and Ostras Beach Club
a posh nightlife on the Riviera of Romagnola
Particularly in Riccione and Milano.

Marittima, the Riviera is an unending string of nightclubs and parties. On the nicest beaches in Italy or in the neighboring hills, where some of the most renowned clubs are located, you may have fun here every single day.

Nothing compares to Riviera Romagnola's stunning beaches and nightlife in Italy. Elegant pubs and clubs that provide all you need for a memorable night out in Italy are wonderful places to spend your time.
Cocorico, Villa delle Rose, and Papeete are places you must see.

Part one

A macroregion of Italy made up of its southern areas is known as Southern Italy, sometimes known as Meridione or Mezzogiorno.

Today, the term "Mezzogiorno" refers to areas that are connected to the people, lands, or cultural heritage of the historical and cultural region that was once politically governed by the former Kingdoms of Naples and Sicily (officially known as Regnum Siciliae citra Pharum and ultra Pharum, or "Kingdom of Sicily on the other side of the Strait" and "across the Strait") and later shared a common organization into Italy's largest pre

History

Greeks started to settle in Southern Italy in the eighth and seventh century BCE for a variety of reasons, including demographic crisis (famine, overpopulation, etc.), the hunt for new economic outlets and ports, and deportation from their country. Greek colonies were also created during this time in locations that were far apart from one another, including Eastern Libya, Massalia (Marseille), and the eastern shore of the Black Sea.

On the Italian Peninsula's southern tip and in Sicily were also included. The Ausones, Oenotrians, and Iapyges were the three principal ethnic groups present in Italy when the first Greek immigrants arrived. Primarily with the Iapygian tribes, relations between the Greek settlers and the indigenous peoples were antagonistic at first. They ultimately had a culture and manner of life influenced by the Hellenic people.

Magna Graecia (Latin for "Great Greece") was the name given by the Romans to the region of Sicily and coastal Southern Italy because it was so densely populated by Greek colonies. However, ancient geographers disagreed on whether the term should also refer to Sicily or just Apulia and Calabria; Strabo was the most well-known proponent of the broader definitions.

Greek culture was transported to Italy via this colonization, including its dialects of the Ancient Greek language, its rituals, and its autonomous polis customs. Eventually mixing with the indigenous Italic and Latin civilizations, an original Hellenic culture quickly emerged. The Greek alphabet's Chalcidian/Cumaean variant, which the Etruscans adopted, was the most significant cultural exchange; the Latin alphabet, which replaced the Old Italic alphabet as the most commonly used alphabet in the world, later developed from the Old Italic alphabet.

During the Middle Ages, the majority of the Greek residents of Magna Graecia were completely Latinized, but there were still certain areas where Greek culture and language persisted and are still used today. As an example, consider the Griko people of Calabria (Bovesia) and Salento (Greca Salentina), some of whom continue to practice their Greek language (Griko language) and traditions. The only remaining remnant of the Greek components that formerly made up Magna Graecia is the language of the Griko people.

Pyrrhus of Epirus's unsuccessful effort to halt the expansion of Roman hegemony in 282 BCE resulted in the south coming under Roman rule, which stayed in place until the arrival of the barbarian invasions (the Gladiator War being a prominent example of the imperial suzerainty being suspended).

After Rome fell in the West in 476, it was returned to Eastern Roman power in the 530s, and some kind of imperial rule persisted until the 1070s. With Zotto's victory in the latter part of the sixth century,

Lombard's hegemony over the whole East was gone.

Culture

Beginning most prominently with Greek colonization, the areas of Southern Italy had certain historical effects that were distinct from those experienced by the rest of the peninsula. Until Latinization was complete during the reign of the Roman Principate, Greek influence dominated the South. Especially with the conquests of Justinian and the Byzantine Empire, Greek influences were revived by the late Roman Empire.

Aspects of Arab culture were transmitted to Italy and Europe through Sicily, which had a unique Norman-Arab-Byzantine civilization during the Middle Ages. Sicily was later conquered by Muslims and made into an Emirate. The Venetians developed colonies as commerce with Byzantium and the Near East flourished, while the Byzantines,

Lombards, and Franks fought it out for control of the remaining mainland.

Most of the South practiced Eastern rite (Greek) Christianity before the Norman invasions in the 11th and 12th centuries. The architecture, religion, and high culture of the area were profoundly influenced by the Norman settlers who came to Sicily and Southern Italy in the Middle Ages. Later, the nascent European nation states—first the Crown of Aragon, then Spain, then Austria—came to control Southern Italy. Being in control of the South for more than three centuries had a significant influence on its culture.

For more than 15 centuries, Jewish communities coexisted in Sicily and Southern Italy. However, in 1492, King Ferdinand II of Aragon issued an edict that forbade Jews from residing there. The number of Jewish Sicilians in the island's population at their peak was probably approximately one-tenth. After the Edict, some of them went to the Ottoman Empire and other locations in Italy and Europe, and they partly converted to Christianity. The majority of these street musicians from Basilicata went on to become professional instrumentalists in symphony orchestras, particularly in the United States, throughout the 19th century when they started to travel the globe in search of riches.

Major tourist destinations in Southern Italy include the Palace of Caserta, the Amalfi Coast, Pompeii, the Sassi di Matera, the Trulli of Alberobello, and numerous ancient monuments (many of which are protected by UNESCO). In Southern Italy, there are also a lot of ancient Greek towns that date back centuries before the founding of the Roman Republic, including Sybaris and Paestum. The country has various national parks that protect some of its beaches, forests, and mountains. The Pollino, which is located between Basilicata and Calabria and is home to Italy's biggest national park, is a notable example.

Traditions and music from Southern Italy, such as the Tarantella and the Neapolitan song, have recently seen a comeback.

Religion

A growing range of religious practices, beliefs, and denominations, together with the supremacy of Christianity, define Italian religion. In Italy, the Catholic Church, whose headquarters are in Rome's Vatican City, is the religion of choice for the majority of people. Beginning in the first century, Christianity was practiced in the Italian Peninsula.

58% of Italians place a very or relatively high value on religion, according to the 2017 Being Christian in Western Europe study by Pew. In the study, only Italy had more Christians who were actively involved in their religion than those who were not.] The third-highest weekly church attendance rate in the European Union, after Poland and Ireland, is in Italy. Francis of Assisi and Catherine of Siena are the patron saints of the Italian Catholic Church.

Arts and Architecture

Without even a cursory look at the surrounding architecture, a journey to Italy would be incomplete. There is an extraordinarily wide spectrum of architectural styles, if you look attentively (or maybe not even that closely).

Roman architecture is present, of course, and is found all across the nation, not only in Rome. There are also several amazing gothic churches, such as the Duomo di Milano and Duomo di Orvieto, both of which have stunningly opulent façade. Even Bavarian Baroque, with German influences, can be seen in German-speaking Bolzano, a

Dolomite city that has an Austrian rather than an Italian feel to it.

As you go south, you first see alpine-green meadows with cows, pine woods, and apple orchards. Then, in the Pianura Padana, you come across arable farmland. Next, you pass through vineyards and tomato fields. Finally, as you approach the very south of the peninsula, you come across olive trees. Even still, as you go farther south, it doesn't only look like the landscape is changing hue; it also seems as if the houses are becoming whiter and lighter.

You'll notice the contrast if you take the seven-hour train ride directly from red-brick "La Rossa" Bologna to sandy-colored Lecce or contrast Modena with Ostuni: one is a mix of reds, yellows, and oranges, surrounded by miles of (mostly beige) farmland in September, and about as far from the sea as you can get in Italy. The Adriatic Sea can barely be seen peeking through between the olive orchards on the opposite side, which is all white and beige and contrasts well with it. Along with being darker than those in the northern cities, the structures in Campania, Calabria, and Sicily. Naples stands out for having an almost yellow light across the whole city.

However, the mood of these structures is derived from the architectural style—the very fussy and showy Baroque—which has to do with the choice of stone and what was locally accessible at the time of construction. Southern Italy's color is mostly a result of these factors. After the Protestant Reformation, the Catholic church made an effort to regain its prominence in society, and this effort culminated in the development of Baroque architecture, a subset of the larger Baroque movement in art and design, which gained traction in Italy towards the end of the 16th century.
The construction of a flamboyant, spectacular façade was done to amaze the

populace, praise the Catholic faith, and entice people to attend church again. Even while there are still some beautiful Romanesque and Gothic structures in the south, the majority of the churches and, in my opinion, the most striking façade are Baroque.

The Baroque architectural style may be found across the nation, but as you go down the peninsula, you'll see a greater concentration of Baroque structures. (A few prominent examples in the north include the Venice Basilica of Santa Maria Della Salute and St. Peter's Cathedral in the Vatican.)

Part two

Transportation

Train

View the beautiful Italian landscape while traveling by train.

Due to the enormous rail network that runs the whole length of Italy, frequent train services link the majority of important cities, including Rome, Florence, Naples, Bologna, and Palermo. The best part is that in between them, you may relax and enjoy the stunning environment.

While a small number of high-velocity services are managed by independently owned Italo, the great majority of trains are operated by Trenitalia, Italy's national railway operator.

Buses

Italy has a vast rail network, yet many places are still inaccessible by railway. The gap between communities that are either too tiny or too far apart to have railway stations is covered by suburban buses.

Boats

While traghetti (smaller ferries) and aliscafi (hydrofoils) transport passengers to and from the smaller islands, navi (big ferries) go to Sicily and Sardinia. Contrary to hydrofoils, most ferries transport automobiles. Travelers may often reserve a two- to four-person cabin or a poltrona, an armchair a la airline, on long-distance boats. Only certain boats offer deck class, which enables passengers to relax or sleep on deck.

Taxis

Near bus and rail terminals, taxis may be obtained. The meter often starts running when you make the call for a radio taxi rather than when you are picked up. The reputation of taxi drivers in popular tourist areas is not good, so be careful to inquire in advance about the fare, if you can pay with a card, and whether the meter is on.

Maximum independence is achieved while traveling by vehicle, motorbike, or Vespa.

Having your car in Italy allows you to drive at your own speed and explore areas with little access to public transit unless you want to stay in art cities. This is especially useful in remote areas like the highlands, islands, and rural areas where there aren't many operating buses.

Accommodations

Gutkowski Hotel

Taking up two 19th-century palazzi, with their evocatively faded pastel façades, situated on the picturesque Lungomare Levante, gazing out to the open sea and sky.

Urban minimalism, beachcomber chic, designer vintage, and upcycled brico are all seamlessly combined to create this one-of-a-kind look. A magnificent roof patio is also present.

Sant'Andrea Belmond Villa

What started as a Cornish engineer's coastal cottage in Sicily is now an immaculate, understated luxury. It is situated on a beach below the storied hill-town resort of Taormina and is surrounded by subtropical gardens. It is the perfect option for anybody looking to combine beach days with sightseeing, culture, and nightlife.

Villadorata Seven-Room Inn

Seven Rooms Villadorata, a breathtakingly beautiful feast for the senses located in a wing of Sicily's most opulent Baroque villa, is the genuine deal. The word "boutique hotel" may no longer have any meaning.

Resort Sant'Angelo

A five-star hotel with stunning views from many of its 21 rooms and suites, the Hotel Sant'Angelo is located in Matera's historic center. The hotel, which was formerly "sassi" cave houses, combines traditional chambers carved out of rock with beautiful villa architecture. We like the vistas, towering ceilings, and beds carved from limestone. Local food is the restaurant's specialty.

The Civita Grotte

Another hotel that manages to be both opulent and exquisite, while also being made from a collection of cave houses carved from the limestone Matera is built, is Le Grotte della Civita. There are 18 unique rooms and suites, all of which include domed caverns, log stoves, and stunning bathrooms with stand-alone bathtubs. Although it serves good food and has culinary workshops, the fine restaurant has the atmosphere of a medieval stronghold. Le Grotte surely has awe-inspiring qualities.

Margherita's Palace

Francis Ford Coppola is the owner of the magnificently renovated Rococo house known as The House Margherita, located in the tranquil village of Bernalda. Its nine rooms, which are chic and well-furnished with both rustic and glitzy elements, provide a true retreat from the hectic world outside. Each one of them is distinct, and they are all arranged around a central courtyard that is dotted with beds of lavender and rosemary. Additionally, you may eat in the lovely kitchen or the patio. You are just 20 minutes from the seaside and there is a private theater and pool.

The Monastery Inn

Located in a former monastery within the historic Aragonese Castle, the atmospheric, tranquil, and chic boutique hotel is positioned atop a rocky outcrop and linked to the island of Ischia by a precarious causeway. Although the ancient monks' cells' bedrooms are basic, the panoramic terrace is one of the island's most romantic locations.

San Cassiano's Don Totu.

For day visits to Lecce, Castro, and Gallipoli, this beautiful townhouse in a peaceful community makes the ideal home base. The old home is much larger inside than it seems from the exterior, with lush grass extending behind the main structure, a pool (with an open, vibrant pool house), and many rooftop terraces.

There are just a few rooms, but each has a casually elegant Italian décor, with ceramic lamps, mid-century furniture, and no TVs. The art-loving academics who oversaw the renovation had an immaculate taste. Beach bags are available to start your seaside trip, and Vespas and bicycles are waiting for you to borrow.

Restaurants

Martina Franca's Trattoria delle Ruote

This location has long been trapped in a temporal loop. The recipes and preparations, as well as the menu, are precisely the same as they were fifty years ago. Eating at Trattoria delle Ruote is a ritual that should not be hurried. Due to the restricted number of tables, customers are recommended to take their time. The unique atmosphere of the rustic environment is enhanced by the tight fit of the tables within a little trulli ornamented with antiquated equipment. Like the surroundings, the cuisine is simple and rustic. You'll start with handmade salumi and formaggi from nearby farms that taste of the Pugliese countryside, then go on to flawlessly thick orecchiette and bouncy balls of creamy mozzarella.

From the pickles to the pasta, everything is cooked on-site, even the herbal liqueurs that linger on the table next to the little bill.

Messapica, Ceglie Cibus

Cibus is situated in an old monastery from the fourteenth century, with stone walls and lime-painted arches, in the backstreets of Ceglie Messapica. A husband and wife team who see food as both a source of enjoyment and a method to learn about a place's culture and history are the ones who gave the restaurant life. Every dish demonstrates a focus on experimenting with various partnering options while using the wonderful ingredients on offer. Before the phrase "zero-mile produce" was even a thing, Cibus was already practicing hyper-locality. Save room for the veal roasted in the stone oven as you work your way through the antipasti and pasta dishes while relaxing beneath the vines. To end, indulge in the extremely sticky biscotti veggies, which are almond cookies filled with jam.

Fasano's Restaurant, Silvio

Ristorante da Silva seems like a well-kept secret among those in the know with an almost nonexistent internet trace. Sitting at their table is like being an extended member of the family for the evening, with Silve on the floor and his mother Maria in the kitchen.

The modest but well-considered meal honors Fasano's history while also including their original perspective. Think tender cow cheeks that fall off the bone, spicy rockets with burrata over cavatelli, and gelato prepared with extra virgin olive oil and honey. Finish the meal off with a cold glass of Silve's handmade digestivo, which is created with chamomile and black pepper. Ristorante de Silve fits well with the design-conscious style for which Puglia is quickly becoming recognized. The restaurant's décor enhances the sense of eating with family, although one with a taste for fine furnishings.

Pizzo and Pizzo

Pizzo & Pizzo, a charcuterie and cheese shop well known for its excellent assortment, is situated just off Via Libertà next to the Politeama Theatre. It also offers excellent beef dishes. a well-liked setting for an evening aperitivo.

Quattro Mani Restaurant

A stunning restaurant with a meal that is inviting and a superb wine list that seems both current and classic. Very strongly advised.

Italian cuisine

Without a doubt, if you were to list the most well-known Italian dishes in the world, many of them would likely originate from the South: pizza, carbonara, and ice cream are just a few examples.

A lot of common misconceptions about Italian culture come from the South of Italy. For instance, picture the stereotypical Neapolitan guy singing fervently in the streets and devouring his Margherita pizza while gesturing with his hands to try to carry on a conversation. Of course, this is only a cliché, but it serves to highlight how rich in cultural imagery and traditions the South of Italy is.

Caciocavallo

The oldest cheese ever manufactured is caciocavallo. Agnone, Capracotta, and Vastogirardi's communities may be proud of it. Caciocavallo is a raw cow's milk product with a firm rind, a straw-yellow color, and a tendency to become brown as it ages.

Pizza marinara

Pizza Margherita, arguably the most well-known representation of Italian food, is the Queen. Pizza is unquestionably far older than Italy itself, embodying the national colors!

Pastiera Italiana

Pastiera Napoletana is a custard-based classic dessert that comes from Naples. An elegant ricotta cream filling and icing sugar topping is called for in the traditional recipe for small crust pastry. Pastiera is considered to be a modern emblem of life and rebirth, perhaps as a result of origin tales.

Taralli Pugliesi

A culinary emblem of Puglia's regional cuisine is taralli pugliesi. The only ingredients used to make these ring-shaped hard crackers are flour, water, white wine, and a few fennel seeds for a fresh flavor.

'Nduja

The 'nduja, an extremely soft and spicy sausage produced of fat, bacon, jowl, and less noble portions of the pig, is unquestionably the first symbol of Calabrian cuisine. It is heavily spiced and given its recognizable brilliant red color by the use of chili pepper.

Los Sardellas

Sardella is just a blend of 'nduja and tiny local fish that has been spiced with chili pepper and fennel. It is often referred to as

"the fish 'nduja" or "caviar of the south."
This regional specialty from the South pairs
well with a hot glass of red or white wine
and has a flavor that is notably robust and
distinctively spicy.

Arancino

In the extensive list of regional food icons,
Arancino unquestionably deserves to be at
the top. Arancini are rice balls that are
breaded, fried, and filled with a
mouthwatering ragù sauce.

Indeed, throughout the years, the
community has been split between those
who name it arancino, as in Catania, and
those who call it arancina, as in the Palermo
region, due to these little and tasty treats.

Norma's Pasta

The most perfect example of basic,
wholesome, and nutritious food, according
to all accounts, is pasta alla Norma. The star

of this meal, originally served with rigatoni pasta, are the sautéed eggplants that are simmered in a thick, garlicky tomato sauce with the pasta.

Top Attractions

Aroc Magno

Arco Magno is without a doubt one of the most beautiful natural wonders in Southern Italy (and that's saying a lot!). If you're in the region, don't miss the secret beach and stunning rock arch in Calabria, which are close to the little hamlet of San Nicola Arcella.

A little stretch of sandy beach is hidden among the rising sea cliffs and craggy, rugged headlands of this Tyrrhenian Sea coastline. They are a part of the Riviera dei Cedri, and by only allowing the waves and sunlight to enter via the twenty-meter-high arch, they form an amazing natural amphitheater.

Naples

Naples, the biggest city in the south, is home to a very diverse history, culture, and cuisine that you should explore. Its evocative streets are home to a variety of artistic and architectural gems despite being rather dirty and run-down.

Impressive locations may be found here, including the massive Castel Nuovo, the charming Royal Palace, and its opulent, fresco-covered church. In addition, there are several eye-catching cathedrals and museums across the huge metropolis, as well as an unending supply of delicious Neapolitan pizza.

Its gleaming coastlines and the towering big Vesuvius in the background hint at all the other magnificent locations you might see. These include the huge ruins at Pompeii and Herculaneum as well as the sun-kissed Sorrento, Capri, and Amalfi Coast.

Maratea

The flashy hamlet of Maratea, affectionately dubbed the "Pearl of the Tyrrhenian," stands in stark contrast to the large, grimy metropolis. It is located in a picturesque area on Basilicata's west coast, nestled in a beautiful valley between mountains and hills covered in forest.

Maratea is not known as "the town with 44 churches" for nothing, and its variety of landscapes, scenery, and vistas alone make it worthwhile to visit. You will often come across their lovely, deteriorating façade and alluring architecture as you explore its spectacular medieval center. The city's major church, Santa Maria Maggiore, was constructed in 1505 and has some intriguing artwork. Watch out for the Statue of Christ that is located atop Mount San Biagio far above the town.

Castelmezzano

The picturesque village of Castelmezzano is situated in a location that is much more breathtaking. Its collection of brightly colored homes, which are rightfully regarded as "one of the most beautiful villages in Italy," is a breathtaking sight when seen in conjunction with the mountains and woods that tower above them.

The secluded village, which is equally distance from Bari and Naples, is tucked away in the impressive-looking Dolomiti Lucane Mountains. You will eventually find the eleventh-century village situated high on the mountainside after traveling inland for around two hours from either. With its well-protected passage, which was established by the Normans who were escaping the advancing Saracens, brigands subsequently used it as a hideout.

You may trek and climb around the nearby mountains in addition to taking pictures of its spectacular background and buildings from different angles. The Seven Stones Path up to the cliff-side Pietrapertosa is a particularly well-liked one. Instead, you should attempt its exhilarating "Flight of the Angel" if you're a little bit of an adrenaline addict. The zipline, which is suspended 100 meters in the air, propels you between the twin cities at a speed of 120 km/h.

Capri

Capri paints a beautiful image with its emerald green hills, towering cliffs, and sparkling blue waves. The island and all of its charming villages, which were once a favorite getaway for Roman emperors, are today one of Southern Italy's most well-liked day trip destinations.

Its mountainous landscapes are easily accessible from Naples and Sorrento, and they already look amazing from the boat trip there. Once there, you may use a funicular to ascend to Capri Town, where you can explore the upscale shops and eateries or go for a walk around the slopes. The villas of Emperor Tiberius, Jovis, and San Michele, are only two of the fascinating historical sites that may be visited.

Pompei and Herculaneum

Pompeii and Herculaneum, two of the most well-known and intriguing archaeological sites in the world, must undoubtedly be visited if you have the opportunity. All of their unearthed streets, villas, and temples are remarkably well-preserved and provide a fascinating glimpse into ordinary Roman life thousands of years ago.

Coasts of Amalfi

Of course, the famous Amalfi Coast cannot be missed. It has long been a very well-liked resort for jet setters and is justly acclaimed for its magnificent Mediterranean vistas and lovely colorful villages that fall over the cliffs.

The southern edge of the Sorrentine Peninsula is bordered by steeply sloping mountains and little fishing towns that overlook the dazzling Gulf of Salerno. Together, they create an unfathomably lovely scene with breathtaking vistas that can be enjoyed all along the shore.

Discreet Gems

Secret hiking routes and ethereal landmarks in Castelmezzano

Castelmezzano is undoubtedly one of Italy's hidden jewels and one of the most stunning locations in Southern Italy. It is worthwhile to go to this less well-known mountain town since it has a laid-back vibe and provides a great chance to see authentic Italian culture without being overrun by tourists.

Clear waters and secret swimming holes may be found in Otranto.

Otranto is the ideal destination to spend cool beach days since it is conveniently located near walking paths, gorgeous, and delightfully brimming with Adriatic Sea vistas. In Puglia's Salento area, Otranto is well known for its castle, quaint old city, and beaches.

A good chunk of the town is encircled by the Lungo mare in Otranto, which is the ideal location to watch the sunset.

Trani is a quaint beach community that avoids commercial tourists.

The finest place to start your exploration of the various beaches and noteworthy sites along the Adriatic Sea coast is Trani.

Monopoli is home to beautiful beaches and historical landmarks.

The city is lovely and deserves a visit even if it is hidden from major tourists.

The frescoed Palmieri Palace, the baroque Monopoli Cathedral, the archaeological museum with ancient graves, and the 16th-century Castle of Carlo V are all worth seeing. With its pastel-colored homes and vintage Fiat 500s parked along the winding lanes, even strolling around town seems like traveling back in time.

The ideal way to see the beaches in Monopoli, Puglia, is to hire a bike and ride along the coastal bike route. Monopoli is home to some of Puglia's greatest beaches.

Ostuni is a little-known whitewashed town in Puglia.

Beautiful Ostuni is in Puglia and is a Citta Bianca or White Town.

Beautiful whitewashed homes and old city walls surround this fortified hilltop village.

One of Southern Italy's hidden beauties, the lovely Ostuni with its understated white beauty.

The most prominent structure in the historic center is Ostuni's Gothic-style Cathedral, which has a beautiful frontal rose window. The town also contains several lovely palaces that are owned by former local nobility in addition to the magnificent cathedral.

There are further locations.

- Ginosa: Cave dwellings in Puglia and Primitivo wine
- The less well-known Amalfi Coast town is Vietri Sul Mare.

- A popular location for foodies on the Sorrento peninsula is Sant'Agata sui Due Golfi.
- Scilla is a hidden gem for cultural and beach lovers in Calabria.
- Ancient history enthusiasts should visit Paestum, a UNESCO site.

Part three

Southern Italy's events

Carnevale

During the Carnevale, Italy is lavishly adorned to mark the beginning of Lent, a time when Christians abstain from meat consumption and other forms of festivity. This celebration presumably has origins that date back to a Pagan celebration in the 12th century. Parties, parades, and masquerade balls are held in many Italian towns to keep the populace amused. Tourists may find it expensive to attend the balls, but you can still take in free street acts, music, and boat parades.

Festa di San Gennaro: The San Gennaro Festival

Dedicated to Saint Januarius, patron saint of Little Italy in New York and Naples, the Festa di San Gennaro is a Neapolitan and Italian-American holiday. According to the Catholic Church's calendar, his feast day is September 19.

La Notte della Taranta: taranta's night

The most significant touring festival, "La Notte della Taranta," will be set up from August 4 to August 26 for its 24th iteration. It's one of the most eagerly anticipated occasions in Salento. Musicians and dancers will go to Puglia for the first time, as well as to towns like Taranto and Alberobello, which are located north of Salento. Melpignano, where the festival's grand finale performance is scheduled on August 28, will serve as its epicenter.

La Notte della Taranta is dedicated to advancing and promoting the folk music heritage, which combines various musical genres including rock, jazz, and symphonic music. The Pizzica, a dance that has come to represent our traditional identity and has spread beyond Puglia's boundaries, is unquestionably the genuine highlight of these summer evenings.

Festival of St. Nicholas: Festa Patronale di San Nicola

The festivities for Saint Nicholas, the patron saint of Bari, take place on May 8 and are a deeply felt occasion across Puglia. In a parade through the city's historic district, more than 60 people carry the saint's relics as they remember the valiant act of the sailors who saved and transported them from Myra to Bari.

The lay celebration of this religious holiday, which includes music and food booths where you may sample local delicacies from Apulian heritage, cannot be separated from it. Saint Nicholas is not just a saint in the traditional sense of the term, but it is also the Festival par excellence, a riot of colors, a blaze of lights, a victory of carousels, and a celebration of traditional gastronomy.

The Focara di Sant'Antonio Abate

Sant'Antonio the Abbot's bonfire is celebrated in Novoli as the Focara di Sant'Antonio Abate.

From January 16 to 18, Novoli, Salento, will host this yearly celebration. A 25-meter-long, enormous bonfire, known as a "focara" in Apulian, is lit here. The populace gathers hay and vine bundles, which are used to fuel the bonfire over the whole month of December until it is lit. Without any lighting, the show is assured, which is a very large bet for a spectacular outcome.

However, how are the saint and the fire-related? To steal fire and warm people's lives across the globe, Saint Anthony the Abbot is said to have descended into hell with his little, obedient pig.

Suggestions for traveling

Packing your baggage for the tube shouldn't be forgotten.

Alternatively, if you're driving, be ready for Italian traffic. Italy's cities each have their distinct public transport system, which often comprises buses, trams, or metro. Studying how to get about the area you're going is an excellent idea if you want to depend on more than just your two feet. Additionally, since many cities provide day tickets, conducting a little study might enable you to make financial savings. The railway network links every major city as well as a few smaller ones.

Learn a little Italian.

Do not assume that everyone speaks English. In Southern Italy, English is not widely spoken, unlike in many other regions of Europe where it is widely spoken along with around ten additional languages for good measure.

Learn a few simple Italian phrases, such as good morning (buongiorno), farewell (ciao), please (per favore), and thank you (grazie), as well as the names of your favorite meals (vino e pasta, please). But don't worry; even if they may not understand your language, the people in the southern region of Italy will go out of their way to be kind and kind to make you feel at home and cared for.

The view is magnificent. You'll most likely need to fly into Rome and take a picturesque train trip of three to five hours along the coast to arrive in Southern Italy. I was reminded of California by the hills, mountains, and pine trees that line Italy's western coast. But think about California with its ruins. Also, castles.

Nonetheless, avoid paying more for first class. If you go during peak season, it's not worth the additional money and you could even have to wait in a queue.

Appropriate gear.

Nobody wants to struggle up 100 stairs in Amalfi or over unsteady cobblestones in any Italian city while carrying heavy luggage. If you want to shop while you're here, bring less than you think you'll need! also, keep an eye on the weather. Even while summer and winter temperatures are usually hot and frigid, you should be ready for changes in the weather if you're traveling in the autumn or spring. Keep in mind that it might turn cold; shorts cannot be worn all year round.

To do your shopping, go to the markets.

Recognize the many Italian regions.

Don't follow the crowd!

With reasonable expectations in mind, plan your excursions and sightseeing.

When you reach there, be sure to withdraw some money from an ATM. When traveling through Southern Italy, don't rely on your debit or credit cards to function; instead, bring enough cash with you!

At the bar, sip your coffee while standing. Sitting is for Americans and visitors. You have to finish your espresso while uncomfortably stooping at the bar in less than five minutes, or you'll have to pay a fine.

A common American falsehood is paninis. It is referred to as a panino in

Italy and is a very straightforward sandwich made with bread, cheese, and meat. It isn't warm and melted. There is too much bread and not enough other things to eat since it is chilly and dry.

Everything is closed from noon till five o'clock. In the south of Italy, avoid attempting to have a late lunch. By the time supper arrives you'll just be ravenous and agitated. Particularly if it's a Sunday since dining establishments are closed all day on Sundays beginning at 1 o'clock. If not, you're screwed. Hopefully, your nonna will prepare you supper or you'll remember to go food shopping.

Whatever the chef is serving that day, please order it. Asking what it is won't help. Never request substitutes. You'll eat it and like it, since it's the freshest item on the menu.

Numerous tunnels may be found. It takes a lot of rising, descending, curving, and other maneuvers to drive across the mountains in the USA. Never in Italy. Mountains in southern Italy can't stand in the way of a motorway; instead, a series of about a million tunnels cut straight through them.

It's not required to tip. You're not required to do it. Not even little. potentially, by offering, you could insult your server. Save your Euros; your tip is already included in the cost of your meal.

For bathroom usage, no purchase is necessary. Even if you don't make a purchase, it doesn't appear to matter if you go inside someone's house, business, or restaurant to use the loo.

Someone may believe you're a tourist if they offer you poor cuisine or give you subpar groceries. They presume that you are uneducated. You have every right to decline their subpar meals and/or goods and demand the high-quality items they provide to everyone else if you do know better.

The beaches are wonderful. The beaches in southern Italy are among the greatest in the whole nation; the sand is smooth and white, and the sea is warm, clear, and vividly blue.

Advice about safety

There are several ongoing wildfires in Italy and many regions are experiencing extreme heat, including Sicily. If you're traveling in a region where there are wildfires, plan on experiencing travel delays. For the most recent information, speak with your travel agency. Keep an eye on the news for updates and heed the guidance of local authorities.

Minor crimes are frequent. Pickpockets and bag snatchers should be avoided while traveling and in tourist areas, especially at busy railway stations. Thieves often operate in teams aboard trains. Look after your possessions.

Political targets are sometimes bombed. Stay away from demonstrations and crowds. follow regional news.

Keep an eye out for terrorist activity. Cities throughout Europe have been attacked by terrorists, as have transit hubs and tourist attractions. heed the advice of authorities.

There are earthquakes and volcanic eruptions in Italy. Landslides and avalanches are caused by powerful earthquakes. Between June and September, forest fires often occur. Follow the guidance of local authorities while keeping an eye on the media.

Call 112. If you need emergency medical care. There are available English-speaking operators.

If you trash, eat, drink, or sit near places of worship or other public structures, you might be punished. Follow the directions on the signage about behavior.

Some cities, like Rome, forbid organized bar crawls.

Photographing government structures and military installations is prohibited. Consult your neighborhood's authorities beforehand.

Avoid purchasing counterfeit goods from unscrupulous street sellers. The law forbids it.

Conclusion

To sum up, traveling across Southern Italy reveals an enthralling tapestry of history, culture, and natural beauty that makes a lasting impression on every traveler. This alluring area, distinguished by its pleasant weather, picturesque scenery, and rich past, provides an immersive experience that appeals to history buffs and leisure seekers alike.

Southern Italy offers a wide selection of activities, from the breathtaking Amalfi Coast to the ancient districts of Naples. Foods like pasta, pizza, and gelato are prominent in the region's culinary scene, which is a highlight. Visitors are welcome to savor these culinary treats while taking in the scene of the quaint towns and the turquoise ocean.

Southern Italy's architecture is strongly rooted in its past, as seen by Pompeii's ancient ruins, the splendor of Matera's cave houses, and the Lecce's Baroque splendor. Each location provides a look into a different era of civilization and the rich history of the area.

The people's friendliness and kindness add even more value to the tourist experience. Travelers may create lasting relationships and get a greater understanding of the authenticity of the region by becoming involved with local culture, whether it is via customary festivals, markets, or just mingling with amiable locals.

Southern Italy's slower pace of life is a breath of fresh air in a world that sometimes goes too quickly. It entices tourists to completely savor the present while appreciating the beauty of their surroundings and the ease of everyday living.

In conclusion, a trip to Southern Italy is more than just a vacation; it's a transforming journey through history and culture. Travelers will remember their experience in the area long after they have left it, thanks to its unique combination of natural beauty, gastronomic pleasures, historical riches, and friendly community spirit.

Printed in Great Britain
by Amazon

31856999R00050